Great Verse
to
Stand Up and Tell Them

by Crawford Howard, Maud Steele,
Bill Nesbitt, Billy Ritchie and
Seamus Lavery

Edited by Doreen McBride

ADARE PRESS
White Gables,
Ballymoney Hill,
Banbridge
Co. Down
Telephone 028 4062 3782

Reprinted 2002
Published by Adare Press
Cover design and illustration by Michael Wibberley
Printed by Textflow Services Limited

ISBN 1 899496 16 5

Great Verse

to stand up and tell them

by Crawford Howard, Maud Steele,
Bill Nesbitt, Billy Ritchie, Seamus Lavery
and Doreen McBride

Edited by
Doreen McBride

Great Verse to Stand Up and Tell Them

In Ireland the tradition of writing comic verse goes back to the beginnings of history when the Bards of old wrote satires poking fun at their lords and masters, and indeed, anyone who annoyed or amused them. It is a tradition which is alive and well in Northern Ireland, fostered by humorous poetry competitions, such as the 'Bard of Armagh' competition, which aims to encourage the release of wit, humour and satire back into the mainstream.

Locally there is a tremendous amount of creative talent which tends to be taken for granted and remains unappreciated until foreign travel and contact with other cultures broadens perspectives. It is still possible to find informal evenings when people take it in turns to perform and, as the saying goes, 'the craic is mighty!' In situations such as these, people who cannot sing or play a musical instrument can take shelter by reciting a humorous monologue, a useful talent requiring nothing more than a bit of nerve and the ability to memorise a few verses.

The majority of verses in this book were first published in 'Stand Up And Tell Them' and 'Stand Up And Tell Them Some More', local best-sellers now out of print. They were written by locally well known yarnspinners who live in Northern Ireland. They are meant to be shared, to be read aloud, or better still, to be memorised and recited by heart. They are arranged by subject as an aid to choosing a piece to learn to fit an occasion. They provide social comment on the times and depict the light hearted, humorous side of life in Northern Ireland which literature and the media usually ignore. It is hoped they will be shared and enjoyed. The are great verses, so have fun. STAND UP AND TELL THEM.

Doreen McBride
Banbridge 1996

Contents

Matchmaking

The Disillusioned Dreamer

Ye know sometimes, I'm just about scunnered,
Wi' workin' and slavin' all day,
Lookin' after a man and a family,
That gives ye no thanks, and no pay.

When I think of the dreams of me young days,
Floatin' down a long aisle, dressed in white,
Being adored by a handsome young husband,
Who'd rush home to me arms every night.

Boys ye must be clean daft, when ye're youthful,
Tae imagine these dreams will come true,
Ye don't think o' the dishes and nappies,
And nobody tae wash them, but you!

You pitied the successful career girl,
You just thought, 'Och, she can't get a man!'
You even felt that bit superior,
Because you had proved that you CAN!

'But now when she's winin' and dinin',
Or enjoyin' the sunshine in Spain,
And your oul' boy's tuk off wi' his cronies,
You're left in the house, wi' the wean.

When you're chained tae the sink, and it's rainin',
And the weans are all fightin' as well,
Oh, what would you give for her life now?
Or even just half an hour, tae yersel'.

Ye spend yer days cookin' and cleanin'
Ye can't even go to the loo,
Without somebody yellin' for mammy,
Ye would think ye had gone to Peru!

The T.V. is your sole entertainment,
An' when ye get time to look at the screen,
You're over to sleep in five minutes,
And wakenin' up when they're playin' 'The Queen.'

Ye compare your oul' boy wi' the heroes,
An' you'll admit that he's no Movie Star,
But when all's said and done, if you're honest,
Aren't ye better wi' him than J.R.?

When ye view the object of yer passion,
Lyin' snorin' in front of the telly,
Och yer heart would still give a wee flutter,
In spite of his chins and beer belly.

And that face that looks back in the mirror,
Is not all that IT used to be
But he never says one word about it,
At least, well, he disn't tae me.

I suppose I should not be complainin'
But a moan does ye good, by a time,
We're a sight better off than some others,
I thank God we're not on the breadline.

And if I was twenty the morrow,
And had me life over again,
I suppose, I would do, what I'm doin',
I wouldn't be without him or the weans!

Maud Steele

The Taxi

I met a girl at the village hop, she said her name was Nancy.
She really was a smasher, and to her I took a fancy,
I asked her could I take her home, she said that she was willin',
But I had to get a taxi, and it cost me thirty shillin'.

Now, that's a lot of money, so I asked her for the half,
And, boys, but she was stingy, for she turned, and just walked aff.
I had to pay it all meself, it simply wasnae fair,
And surely it was only right that she should pay her share?

Women! Ach, they're all the same, as selfish as can be,
Preyin' on poor eejits, the likes of you and me,
They'd take your last make, so they would, given half the chance,
And take the sting away from it by callin' it 'romance'!

Well, anyway, this Nancy had gone off and left me stranded.
You must admit, her actions were mighty heavy handed,
For that thirty bob was all I had, and och, it made me sick
When the rotten taxi driver wouldnae take me home on tick!

And then the rain came peltin' down, a terrible oul' night,
And I got soaked from head to foot, I must have been a sight.
I walked, and tried to thumb a lift, but nobody would stop,
I tell you, I was scunnered at that stupid village hop!

A good three hours it took me, till I was home in bed,
And, och, the thoughts of vengeance that went runnin' through
    my head!
But, in spite of all the walkin', I found it hard to sleep,
When I thought about that thirty bob, I felt that I could weep!

Well, I saw her at the village hop, time and time again.
A right flirtatious creature, that was brave and plain,
For every week she'd flash her eyes at Tom, or Dick, or Maxie,
And one of them would take her home, and always in a taxi!

9

Well, I let a wheen of months go by, and then I chanced me arm,
And asked to take her home again, with every ounce of charm,
I acted like the memory of that night was far behind me,
And as far as Nancy was concerned, she really couldn't mind me!

Well, we went home in a taxi, for that was Nancy's style,
And it cost me thirty bob again, but I paid up with a smile,
For I'd found that Nancy's father was the man who did the drivin' -
Because of her, his business was absolutely thrivin'!

So I set me cap at Nancy, and her and me got wed.
I'd always sworn to wed a lass who'd got a business head!
And now we've got three daughters, they're beautiful, and sweet,
And I don't own a taxi, I own a bloomin' fleet!

Bill Nesbitt

The Rivals

Whenever I visit a friendly bar
To sample the local ales,
The things I hear
With my eager ear
Inspire my poetic tales.
Many a yarn I've listened to
That's given me great delight,
But none compared
To the one I heard
Down at the pub, last night.

The man on the stool beside me looked
Just a little the worse for wear,
As he turned to me,
"My friend," said he,
"I've a story I'd like to share.
You're a man with a kindly sort of face,
And I know I've got a cheek,
But my burning need
Is great indeed,
And I've simply got to speak!

"You see before you a tortured man,
A being in dark distress,
I've lived for years
In a vale of tears
And deep unhappiness,
And it's all because of a girl I loved,
The fairest in all the land.
Her heart I sought
But a rival fought
For the right to the lady's hand.

"She said that she loved us both the same,
And was torn between the two,
That she couldn't decide
Whose blushing bride
She'd be, or what to do.
And so it was left to the two of us
To sort the thing out right.
And we did, you know,
In a toe-to-toe,
A bloody and bruising fight.

"And that's the reason you see me now,
A man with a broken heart,
A man with an air
Of dark despair,
Whose life has been torn apart."
I said to the man, "I understand.
When love, your life has crossed,
The scars don't heal,
I know how you feel,
And I'm sorry to hear you lost."

He looked at me then with tear stained cheeks,
"It's hard to explain, I guess.
Since that far off night,
When I fought that fight,
I've known great bitterness.
I'm paying the price for my fine romance
And everything I've done,
For that nagging wife
Is the bane of my life.
I didn't lose. I won!"

Bill Nesbitt

Love in the Nineties

'Come all ye fine people
An' listen til me song,
It's only 40 verses
An' will not keep ye long'

The young lass stood at the lamp-post,
The young lass strutted her ass,
She giggled and wiggled and tittered
For she hoped a young lad would pass.

A young lad came up on the highway,
A young lad who was dressed til kill,
Black leathers, Doc. Martens and ear-rings
All designed for a young lass til thrill.

The young lass kept on chewing gum.
The young lass luked at his big tattoo,
The young lass muttered, 'Now how come
I know I fancy the likes of you?'

The young lad gazed on her great wee figure,
Seys he til her, 'Yer stickin' out!
With a lass like you til walk beside me
I sure wud have a lot of clout.'

The young lass flashed him a luk of passion.
Says she til him, 'Yer dead on!
A love like ours never goes out of fashion,
I'll shack up with you from now on!'

They went til live in the townland of Keady,
Where they rented a fine wee house.
They worked til help the poor and needy
Til she found him in bed with another spouse.

She yelled, 'You are an awful disgrace,
In fact you are a terrible disaster,
Throwing my love back in my face!'
Then she went and busted his ghettoblaster!

The young lad flew intil a rage,
He stud and guldered, 'I've had enough!
My life is beginning another page!'
Then he went til luk for another bit of stuff!

The young lass stood at the lamp-post,
The young lass strutted her ass,
She giggled and wiggled and tittered
As she hoped another lad would pass!

Doreen McBride

The Process

Consider, if you will, with me
The act of procreation -
The task we set about, with glee,
For Man's regeneration...
And tell me, husband, tell me, wife -
This deed inspired by Cupid...
Have you ever, in your life
Seen anything more stupid?

You'd think that God, in all His wit
And mighty comprehension
Could surely have improved on it,
This singular invention -
The thought of all the human herd
Indulging in this action
Is one that strikes me as absurd -
I'm dumb with stupefaction!

It starts off with a tender kiss,
Develops into passion -
And, after that, it's hit or miss
In most haphazard fashion...
The logic in this foolish feat,
This striving and this straining,
The sweating skin, the humid heat,
Is quite beyond explaining!

They say it makes the world go round
And sends this planet spinning -
With half a chance, the thing is bound
To tempt saints into sinning,
But I am not a holy saint,
Nor am I hard to tempt,
And, from libido's lustful taint,
I'm nowhere near exempt!

It's just the same with birds and bees
And every other creature -
With fawns and frogs and flies and fleas,
Life's most compelling feature…
And yet I feel that I must say
I've reached the firm deduction -
There should have been a simpler way
Of human reproduction.

The process is uncouth and crude
And highly inefficient
(Though I have done the best I could
To make myself proficient!)…
The whole thing is a tangled mess
And very far from clever -
But yet, you know I must confess….
I wouldn't change it - ever…!

Bill Nesbitt

I wouldn't change it - ever…!

Foreign Travel

Maggie Kilmartin's Trip to Australia

Air : The Blackthorn Stick

Now Maggie Kilmartin from Ballygomartin was fond of her grub
    and as fat as a pig,
For drinkin' and atin' she couldn't be baten from Belfast to Bangor,
    from Cork to Conlig.
Her enormous figure got bigger and bigger
Her weight was in excess of eighty-five stone!
She twisted her ankle one night on the Shankill
And said, "Holy Jesus! I'll never get home!"

There was a terrible sound when oul' Meg hit the ground
And out of the belfreys flew hundreds of bats
The noise it was shockin' and buildings was rockin'
From Tennent Street till the Unity Flats
Then the polis said, "Here! We must get the street clear!
Thon bomb must have weighed more than two hundred pounds!"
Then a fella came runnin' and said, "Don't be funny!
It's Maggie Kilmartin has fell on the ground!"

Now they all tried to lift her, but nothin' could shift her.
She lay like a big stranded whale in the street
The traffic was slowin' and the horns was all blowin'
The polis at last had admitted defeat
So a plan was concerted, the traffic diverted
The polis admitted they hadn't a clue
They said, "This is barmy, we'll send for the army,
We'll see if them fellas 'll know what to do!"

Now the army soon came with a massive great crane
And said, "We'll soon shift her, on that you can swear."
So they started the engine an' pullin' and winchin'
The wheels of the crane went straight up in the air
Then a soldier said, "Maisie! Do you see what I see?
She's sinking right down in a ruddy great 'ole!"
And under oul' Meg the ground started to sag
And she disappeared down like a bloody great mole!

Now as they all feared Maggie disappeared
And they all gathered round to see where she had gone
An' amidst roars of laughter the crane follied after
Wi' polis an' army an' all hangin' on!
They said, "It's a failure, she's away to Australia!
You better give in and give Sydney a ring
For if they can't reject her at least they'll expect her,
To arrive unannounced is a terrible thing!"

With puffin' an' blowin' oul Maggie kept goin'.
An' found at last she was gettin' too warm
She said, "This is shockin', I've burnt my good stockins!
If I had of knew, I would not have put them on!"
But slowly and surely she got to Kalgoorlie
The Australians stood round as the ground it did crack,
And they said, "This old geezer's got no flamin' visa!"
So they hit her a kick and sent her straight back.

Now Meg went back down through the hole in the ground
And soon she was back in the heat and the smoke.
Says she, "This is no go! I feel like a yo-yo!
The heat and the stour here would near make you boke!"
But the funny thing was like, whatever the cause like,
The way these things happens beyond you nor me
She burnt her good sweater but her ankle got better
She leapt out in the Shankill as fit as a flea!

Now my sad tale of woe now, has not long to go now,
For Maggie decided that she would get thin
They gave her a diet, she thought she would try it
So she went and threw all her grub in the bin.
She got wee-er and wee-er till you could hardly see her
She could almost walk through a crack in a door
For want of good 'atin' she slipped through a gratin'
And never was seen in the Shankill no more!

Crawford Howard

For want of good 'atin' she slipped through a gratin'

The Orange "Pilgrims"

The pilgrimage coach came to lift us,
To take us away down to Thurles,
And big Mary Rose from the Springfield
Was proud of her hair set in curls.

We crowded round, some clutching liquor
Especially brought for the trip,
With most bottles already sampled
By considerably more than a sip.

In the midst of us there were two strangers
Whom no one had seen there before
And nobody asked for their tickets
As we all scrambled in through the door.

They just seemed to flop on the back seat
And soon the coach got underway
But we gathered, although they were tipsy,
That their first names were Lily and May.

They just sat and tippled their whiskey,
And to tell you the truth, so did I.
By the time we were crossing the border
A few of the travellers were high.

Then some of us started off singing,
Though Lily and May didn't join,
But they let out a gulder, "Up Billy!"
Just as we crossed over the Boyne.

Soon after we pulled in at Dublin,
A break prearranged to have lunch,
Where Lily and May staggered gaily
And got off with the rest of the bunch.

We straightened up as we assembled,
Though Lil and May cared not the least
And they weren't even slightly embarrassed
When they came face to face with a priest!

Lil says, "Hi! Listen here fella,
'Til I put a word in your ear.
I think you'd be better to scarper,
I doubt if you'll be welcome here!"

The wee priest says, "Pardon me madam,
On your state I don't wish to encroach,
But surely you ought to be sober
Since you're just off a pilgrimage coach."

"Pilgrimage? What?" exclaims Lily,
As a good look around her she made,
"This morning we set off for Bangor,
To go to an orange parade."

Well, hearing amidst the confusion,
"What's all this?" questions big Mary Rose,
Still under effects of the liquor,
You could tell by the red of her nose.

"Now calm down," says Father John Reilly,
"The ladies just made a mistake."
"Mistake is it?" bellowed big Rosie,
"She'd be needing a slap on the bake."

He always remembers the day that
He went for a dip with the girls!

21

"Why you big fenian hussy!" yells Lily,
Making to grab Rosie's throat,
But wee Father John got between them
Which only got on both their goat.

"Well! You oul' orange bitch you," screams Rosie
Ignoring the priest's warning call,
Made a charge and they all lost their balance
And fell into the Royal Canal!

That dampened their urge to do battle
And hastened an end to their war.
Rosie and Lil had to suffer our laughter
While stuck to the oxters in glar.

If looks could have killed I can tell you
They'd have slaughtered the half of the bus,
But the miracle was they stopped fightin'
And directed their venom at us!

We got them fished out and their perfume
Was 'Eau de Canal Bottom Stink'
The saga had not helped appearance
But had countered effects of the drink!

They muttered and cursed as we sniggered
And called them a fine matching pair.
Gone was the make-up from Lily
And the curls had all left Rosie's hair.

A shower, then some lunch and refreshments,
Not to mention a quick change of clothes.
Soon we were ready for leaving.
It was then that a problem arose.

We wanted to make up lost time now,
But what about Lily and May?
We could not leave them stranded in Dublin,
It was best that they came all the way.

Of this they were somewhat reluctant,
But against it they balanced their need,
And not wishing to cause any further delay,
They made a snap choice and agreed.

On arrival at our destination
They came with us, both bold as brass,
Right up to the door of the chapel,
But drew lines at attending the mass.

When back on the coach home to Belfast
Reflecting the chain of events
Rose and Lil thought the whole thing hilarious,
And them from both sides of the fence.

Rosie got great friends with Lily,
And Lily became her best pal,
Though Lil often said, "You're a Baptist
Since that episode in the canal!"

And every time Father John Reilly
Encounters a coach bound for Thurles
He always remembers the day that
He went for a dip with the girls!

Billy Ritchie.

The Four Seasons

Valentine

My love, it saddens me to say
That Valentine has had his day,
And, though it might seem very hard,
This year, I'm sending you no card.

You're wonderful, oh, lover mine -
The archetype of the Lord's design...
When he created you, I'd say
He threw that perfect mould away...

There's no-one in the world like you,
And that is your opinion, too -
Never one to hide your light,
You're Number One ...in your own sight...

You know that you're a raven beauty,
A cuddlesome and comely cutie,
The most alluring man could find
In all the realm of womankind...

Your mirror is your constant friend -
You watch it daily, without end,
Deep in love with your reflection,
Drinking in your own perfection....

You touch your skin, you stroke your hair,
You find yourself exceeding fair,
And smile with pleasure when you feel
The magic of your own appeal...

By yourself, you've been encaptured,
Titillated and enraptured -
The fount of all your inspiration
Lying in self admiration...

You're fascinated and enchanted
By the looks that God has granted -
Quite enamoured with each feature
Of yourself, you lovely creature...

You're everything you've ever dreamed -
You're absolutely self-esteemed -
If you had not been born as you,
I'm sure you would have wanted to!

You find it not the slightest odd
That God has made you so unflawed,
And quite convinced, it seems to me,
You're everything a girl should be...

But all your silly self-adoring
Is beginning to get boring...
If you're so grand, and mighty fine -
Then be your own darned Valentine...!

Bill Nesbitt

Surprise, Surprise

Ye cud 'a knocked me down wi' a feather,
When me oul' boy walked in through the door,
Wi' a Valentine card an' red roses,
Sure I nearly fell down through the floor.

Eighteen Valentines Days I'd kep' hopin',
For some flowers or a card, but no fear,
'Ye don't bother wi' that when ye're married.'
Was his lame oul' excuse every year.

But what's prompted this romantic gesture?
What's he lookin' or what's on his mind?
(Isn't it desperate to be that suspicious)
But the answer I'm anxious to find.

Och maybe all them T.V. adverts,
Have at last filtered through till his brain,
An' persuaded him flowers for the missus,
From yappin' might make her refrain!

But, middle age makes men go—funny!
So, I better just mind what I say,
An' be thankful it's me that's got roses,
Or there'll be none next Valentine's Day!

Maud Steele

St Patrick and the Snakes

You've heard of the snakes in Australia,
You've heard of the snakes in Japan,
You've heard of the rattler—that old Texas battler—
Whose bite can mean death to a man.
They've even got snakes in old England—
Nasty adders all yellow and black—
But in Erin's green Isle we can say with a smile
They're away—and they're not coming back!

Now years ago things was quite different—
There was serpents all over the place.
If ye climbed up a ladder ye might meet an adder,
Or a cobra might lep at your face,
If ye went for a walk up the Shankill,
Or a dander along Sandy Row,
A flamin' great python would likely come writhin'
An' take a lump outa yer toe!

Now there once was a guy called St. Patrick,
A preacher of fame and renown—
An' he hoisted his sails and came over from Wales
To convert all the heathens in Down,
An' he hirpled about through the country
With a stick an' a big pointy hat,
An' he kept a few sheep that he sold on the cheap,
But sure there's no money in that!

He was preachin' a sermon in Comber
An gettin' quite carried away
An' he mentioned that Rome had once been his home
(But that was the wrong thing to say!)
For he felt a sharp pain in his cheek-bone
An' he stuck up a hand 'till his bake
An' the thing that had lit on his gub (an' had bit)
Was a wee Presbyterian snake!

Now the snake slithered down from the pulpit
(Expectin' St. Patrick to die),
But yer man was no dozer—he lifted his crozier
An' he belted the snake in the eye,
And he says till the snake, 'Listen legless!
You'd just better take yerself aff!
If you think that that trick will work with St. Patrick
You must be far worser nor daft!'

So the snake slithered home in a temper
An' it gathered its friends all aroun'
An' it says, 'Listen, mates! We'll get on wer skates,
I reckon it's time to leave town!
It's no fun when you bite a big fella
An' sit back and expect him to die
An' he's so flamin' quick with thon big, crooked stick
That he hits ye a dig in the eye!'

So a strange sight confronted St. Patrick
When he woke up the very next day.
The snakes with long faces were all packin' their cases
An' headin' for Donegall Quay.
Some got on cheap flights to Majorca
And some booked apartments in Spain.
They were all headin' out and there wasn't a doubt
That they weren't going to come back again.

So the reason the snakes left old Ireland,
(An' this is no word of a lie),
They all went to places to bite people's faces
And be reasonably sure that they'd die.
An' the oul' snakes still caution their grandsons,
'For God's sake beware of St. Pat!
An' take yerselves aff if you see his big staff,
An' his cloak, an' his big pointy hat!'

Crawford Howard

Firework Frolics

You can't buy fireworks in Belfast,
They've been banned this few years past,
But none the less you'll hear the din
Of those that have been smuggled in
From places over in the South,
Particularly County Louth.
This tale's of such a smuggler's load.
A lady from the Oldpark Road
Who went, according to the talk
On an excursion to Dundalk.
It being near to Hallowe'en
Decided to procure a wheen
Of squibs and bangers from a store,
And powerful rockets by the score.
Such bit of shopping being done,
Her problems really now begun,
To bring her haul North in one piece
Past customs, army and the police.
The best way seemed to her in haste
Was tie the whole lot round her waist.
Thus she fixed them right around
With all the rockets pointing down,
Made sure that none would slip or flop
By wearing corsets on the top.
With coat pulled tightly round her back,
She looked just like spuds in a sack.
A fancy cape kept out the rain,
Thus clad, she headed for the train.
The journey was without event.
Back in her street she felt content,
Reaching home could now relax,
Having bluffed two army checks.
Stood bragging in her living room,
How they'd be seeing fireworks soon,
Little dreaming as she gloated,

'Twould be sooner than she thought it,
For as she boasted of her ruse
A fire spark lit a rocket fuse,
Which firing threw her on the floor
And zoomed her through the open door.
Thus several others also lit,
Speeding her up quite a bit.
The thrust this gave was quite enough
To, with her cape spread, take right off
With such a great increase in power
To reach a thousand miles an hour.
She realised her path of flight
When going past a satellite,
Creating every way she went
Confusion in the firmament.
Astronomers were on their toes
With wide reports of U.F.O.s,
While worried N.A.S.A. experts met
Computer data prints to vet,
To try and figure out just why
This object swished around the sky.
The Russians looked on in dismay,
With urgent calls to U.S.A.
As jumping jacks began to burn
She took a sudden downward turn,
Coming back t'wards earth again,
Amidst a shower of golden rain,
As homewards o'er the coast she sped
A passing seagull shook its head.
By using cape she tried to steer
With lowered feet, like landing gear,
But catching power lines by her boots
Pulled up two pylons by the roots
Cables touched as through she tore
Causing flashing arcs galore.
While this display lit up the night
People talked of Northern Lights.
Doomsday preachers gazed on high
Declaring that the end was nigh.

Then swooping low, she cut it fine
And cleared the washing off a line,
But over home she felt a pain
And yelled, 'I'll circle round again.
A hose I urgently require,
I'm sure my bloomers are on fire!
Better hurry! Understand?
Before the blaze gets out of hand.
If that should happen I'm afraid
You'll have to call the Fire Brigade.'
They hosed her out the next time round,
And in attempting to touch down
In front of crowds turned out to watch
She landed in a cabbage patch,
But coming just too quickly in
She gouged the lawn up with her chin.
As final rockets fizzled out
The crowds let out a mighty shout.
Dishevelled she lay in repose
Entangled in that line of clothes.
The kids all gave a mighty cheer.
'We hope you'll do the same next year!'

Billy Ritchie

The kids all gave a mighty cheer.
'We hope you'll do the same next year!'

The Santa Claus Syndrome

D'ye see Christmas? It's only a nuisance,
I'm browned aff long before it gets here,
Wi' shoppin' and panickin' and rushin',
An' everything now's got that dear!

The weans have been crakin' for months now,
This whole Santa thing is a cod,
Ye cud run yersel' intae fortune,
Tae convince them it's not a big fraud.

They see all this overpriced rubbish,
Advertised everyday on T.V.
An' it's, 'Mammy, will Santa bring me that?'
Ye wud think that ye got it all free!

There's all this keepin' up wi' the Jones's,
'Wee Jimmy's gettin' a BMX bike,
An wee Laura's gettin' a Cabbage Patch Kid doll,
An' a big pram.' Did y'iver hear the like?

An' John there, he wants a computer,
That costs two hundred poun' maybe more,
An May wants a T.V. for her own room,
Boys, wouldn't weans make yer head sore?

But, I wonder if these fancy presents,
Will bring half the excitement we got,
As we crept down on Christmas mornin'
And discovered our big lumpy sock?

Boys, we danced wi' delight, when we foun' out
That oul' Santa had come after all,
And brought us a sock full of presents,
The more now, they would seem very small.

We would hoke out a pencil and rubber,
A paintbox, a hankie, a book,
A wee bag of gold chocolate money,
An' an apple and orange from the foot.

We were happy wi' these simple items,
The weans now wud say, 'That's not fair!'
But Santa Claus brought us great pleasure,
An' he didn't have tae be a millionaire!

But the weans will grow up in a few years,
An' wi' Santa they'll no longer fuss,
An' Hi! Christmas lost most of its magic,
Since Santa stopped comin' tae us!

So perhaps it IS worth all the bother,
Tae make some of their wee dreams come true,
And give THEM somethin' nice tae look back on
When they're ouler, like me, an like you.

Maud Steele

So perhaps it IS worth all the bother

Happy Christmas Belfast

Father Christmas was sittin' in Iceland,
He lives there, like, everyone knows.
He was toastin' his toes by the fire
And muttering, 'Good luck 'till yez, toes!'
Mrs. Christmas come in wi' a letter.
Says she, 'The post's landed at last!'
Father Christmas took one look and shuddered,
And says 'My God! The post-mark's Belfast

Mrs. Christmas 'rared up' like a tiger.
'You're not going back there no more!
Ye remember what happened ye last time.
Ye arrived back in Iceland half tore!
An' the turkey was burnt to a cinder,
An' you lyin' full in the sleigh,
An' you fell in the arm-chair half stupid,
An' I put the reindeer away.'

Father Christmas looked suitably sheepish,
'I got lost goin' over the hills.
I went down thon big chimney with smoke comin' out,
Sure I didn't know it was Bushmills!
And the heat and the fumes of the whiskey,
An' me only out of my bed,
An' what with one thing an' another,
The whole thing went straight to my head.'

Mrs. Christmas says, 'Bushmills yer granny!
Ye never were there in yer puff!
Ye were rakin' around with them winos in town
Sure ye never could get half enough!
Ye were seen staggerin' 'full' outa Kelly's
Wi' thon three oul' men from the East,
An' you drove the oul' sleigh down Chapel Lane the wrong way,
An' nearly ran over a priest.'

Father Christmas says 'Give us the letter!
I've had just enough of your chat!
You've a tongue on ye worse nor your mother
An' there's not nothin' worser nor that!'
(Father Christmas's grammar was suspect
Though he went to a very good school—
The famous North Pole Comprehensive—
They don't turn out mugs as a rule.)

Father Christmas tore open the letter,
Then he started to laugh like a drain,
An' he says to the wife, 'This'll kill ye!
It's thon wee lad from Belfast again!
Do you know what he's askin' for this time?
It isn't a train or a bike.
He wants me to make them stop fightin'
In Belfast for Christmas, like!'

Mrs. Christmas says 'Make them stop fightin'?
There's no mortal body could do it
But still, though, you'll have to do somethin'
Or else they'll all say you have blew it!
You remember thon bottle of powder
Thon traveller left here thon day?
An' you thought it was only a gimmick
An' it's kickin' about in the sleigh?'

'And the label says, 'Full Strength Peace Powder',
And you sprinkle it over their heads,
An' it makes them feel all 'palsy-walsy'—
At least that's what the traveller said!'
Father Christmas says, 'Heavens, we'll try it!
I'd better get weavin' the day.
Get out there an' harness them reindeer,
An' throw my red suit in the sleigh!'

He was over Belfast in ten minutes.
He travelled so fast it would blind ye!
But as he said, 'Them reindeer can motor
If ye get a good tail wind behind ye!'
But in slowin' down over the city
He just missed a terrible fate.
He was nearly run down by the shuttle
That was comin' in two hours late!

But at last he got into position
And he opened a kind of trap-door,
An' he emptied the bottle of powder
Right down through the hole in the floor,
And as it fell down on the city
The effect was immediate and drastic!
Father Christmas looked down in amazement,
And he says, 'This is fan-flippin'-tastic!'

Father Christmas says
'Give us the letter!

Ian Paisley was sending out Christmas cards,
With tidings of gladness and hope,
And he sent one to Margaret Thatcher
And begod! He sent two to the Pope!
Yes, he sent one to Margaret Thatcher
Saying, 'Dear Maggie, Ulster says "Yes"
And as for your Anglo-Irish agreement;
I hope it's a roaring success!'

Some powder blew right down to Dublin
And it filtered through into the Dail.
Charlie Haughey grabbed Garrett Fitzgerald
And they both did a dance in the aisle.
Then they thought that a drink was in order
So they headed for Guinness's brewery
But Garrett says, 'Charles, get your motor!
The booze is far cheaper in Newry!'

Cardinal O'Fiaich got a sniff of the powder
And he did what you might think was rash.
He decreed that each Catholic church service
Should begin (and conclude) with the 'Sash'.
The Hibernians marched up the Shankill,
The Orangemen marched up the Falls,
Sammy Wilson saluted the tricolour,
And John Hume was bawlin' 'Derry's Walls'.

But up in the sky over Belfast
Father Christmas was chuckling with glee,
As the oul' reindeer started to gallop
An' he headed back home for his tea,
An' he smiled as the city grew smaller
And muttered, 'How long will it last?
But a few days of peace—you deserve it—
So here's "Happy Christmas, Belfast".'

Crawford Howard

Cold Turkey

What the heck do ye do wi' a turkey,
When all the best bits hae been ate?
An' the longer you look at the carcass,
The more an' more scunnered ye get.

But it seems such a pity to waste it,
An' throw it straight out in the bin,
So ye try to compose a new recipe,
Where ye can slip all them oul' brown bits in.

So ye chop up some mushrooms an' onions,
An ye stir up a nice curry mix,
Then ye lob in the turkey left-overs,
And hey presto! a dinner for six!

It's not bad served wi' rice white an' fluffy,
Ye're a cookery genius, that's plain!
The weans take one look at the dinner,
An' say, 'Heavens, not turkey again!'

Maud Steele

Keep Fit

The Fitness Fanatic

If ye want tae survive and be healthy,
Ye must get up and do exercise,
Well, that was the thought that came to me,
When thon big Keep Fit Poster I spied.

It said 7. 30 on Wednesdays,
Come on now and join in the fun,
I vowed to be fitter for Christmas,
So I went to the class and signed on!

A collection of ladies had gathered,
Clad in sportswear of all sorts and kinds,
Some had figures as skinny as beanpoles,
Some had, well, more mature ones, like mine!

A slim young thing appeared on the platform,
Wi' a tape player clutched in her hand,
She outlined all the moves she expected
Us tae do when the music began.

We kicked off wi' a bit o' head rollin',
And joggin' tae loosen our knees,
This isn't too bad, I was thinkin,
For I hadn't even started tae wheeze!

But, 'That's just a warm up,' she told us,
'There's something more strenuous to come,
Just do twenty or so Jumping Jacks now,
And then walk round the floor, on yer bum!'

From that we went on to the stretchin',
And touchin' our hands tae the groun',
And bendin' and rockin' and rollin'
And burlin' our arms roun' and roun'.

Me poor oul legs now were protestin',
But she hadn't finished, Oh no!
It was, 'Down on the floor, stretch your legs up,
And now let them down, very slow.'

We had a short break tae recover,
And I wiped off the sweat from me brow,
Me poor battered body was achin',
I was beginnin' tae regret me rash vow.

The first part was bad, but by hokey!
It was nothin' compared tae the next,
She near killed us wi' skippin' an dancin',
And when nine o'clock came we weren't vexed!

Me face was as red as a beetroot,
And me legs were as limp as a rag,
And back home I managed tae stagger,
And fell back in the bath, like a bag.

By Friday, the oul' joints had stiffened,
I've spent all weekend feelin' a wreck,
But, on Wednesday, I'll dig out me track suit,
And to that Keep Fit, I'll go back!

For ye know, I will not let it beat me,
I'll jog, and I'll skip and I'll run,
And by Christmas NO ONE will be fitter,
When is that Belfast Marathon?

Maud Steele

Aw, Have a Heart!

Looking after ourselves, was what we had in mind,
When we went to the class, and our names we all signed.
We sat on the floor, got to know one another,
And discussed what we hoped this new class had to offer.

We looked for our pulses and felt round and round.
Some felt they had snuffed it, when no pulse they found,
But Mary assured them they'd nothin to fear,
And a digital monitor clipped on their ear.

We talked about eating a healthier diet,
And with Wednesday night zeal, we decided to try it.
We must cut our intake of salt, sugar and fat,
And the faithful oul' chip pan? Well, goodbye to that!

The folly of drinkin' and smokin' we've learned,
And to sensible habits, we no doubt have turned.
We're now reading food labels, instead of good books,
We're starving our minds, to improve on our looks.

We've cut out the drink and the fags—signed the pledge.
We're livin' on 'All Bran' skim milk, fruit and veg,
And while doubtless the value of fibre we're proving,
Some have found the experience, a little TOO moving!

We've clenched up our buttocks, and held tummies in,
And learned to touch walls with our nose or our chin,
We've strengthened our arms, our abdomens and thighs,
With half squats and press ups, loud creakings and sighs!

With a tape and a chart, we have checked body fat,
And discovered we're obese! Well just fancy that!
But when energy levels seemed likely to dip,
Mary passed round the oranges,, to perk us all up.

Then she set pulses racing, with an exercise bike,
Which took us to nowhere and back in one night!
The bench steppin' proved kinda hard on the legs,
But it sure made us glad we weren't still on the fegs!

We've tried joggin' and skippin, we've tried hoppin', too,
But this leaping about made us dash to the loo!
We hope all this effort will make our hearts stronger,
And if we keep it up, perhaps we will live longer.

Then we lay on our backs, and we tried to relax,
And it's hard when your mind keeps on turnin' to snacks,
But when lights were switched off, Mary's voice was so soothing
It took all our will power to keep us from snoozing!

Back home we undid all the good we had done
With a Mars bar or two, or a big fresh cream bun,
But decided, tomorrow we'd stop all this cheating,
And make a serious effort at healthier eating.

We've booklets and leaflets, and charts for the wall,
It'll take us to Christmas to read through them all!
And if dedication, some of us did lack,
Sure we came along anyway, just for the crack!

Maud Steele

Hearty Eating

The Foodaholic

There once was an oul' alcoholic
That lived up the Cliftonville Road.
His behaviour was quite diabolic
An' he niver left 'til he was 'throwed'
Outa every pub in the district
'till the doctor said, 'If ye don't stop
Inside of six months at the latest
You will definitely be for the chop!'

Now this scared the oul' eejit stupid
So' he never went into a pub
But the funny thing was, like, whatever the cause, like,
He began getting drunk on his grub!
Now this was a strange situation
For it he got a mouthful o' tae
or a good bowl of soup his head started to droop
An' the wife would say, 'God, he's away!'

Sez the wife one night, 'See thon oul' grocer?
I'd like to get him by the hair
For he stood thon oul' eejit an onion
An' now he's away on the tear!'
An' you know where they found the oul' geezer?
That full that he couldn't half stan'
Lyin' across a deep freezer
Wi' a fish finger clutched in his han'.

But then he fell into bad company
For he met an oul' fool like himself,
That got rotten on jelly an' custard
Or whatever he pinched off the shelf
And they'd get themselves begfuls o' toffee
An' sit gettin' plastered all day,
Standin' each other black coffee
An' fightin' about which one would pay.

They were soon known all round the district
An' they thought it was terrible hard
If they went in to get a fish supper
They were always told, 'Sorry, you're barred!'
And the poor Chinese waiters would worry
For they all knew just what to expect,
If yer men hit the chow mein and curry
They knew that the whole place would get wrecked!

But one night yer men overdone it.
They had two pasties over the eight
An' they borrowed a car 'till get home, like'
For they knew it was terrible late,
An' of course they were stopped by a peeler
Who started to shout and to 'barge'
An' he says, 'Yez have both done it this time!
Yer arrested for bein' drunk in charge!'

Now the oul' fellas stood up in Court like,
An' they said, 'We have got this rap bate!
Yez have made out the charge sheet all wrong, like,
We were not drunk—we were ate!'
An' ye'll still see them most Sunday mornings
As they wait to get in for a 'cure'
Standin' about with their tongues hangin' out
An' bangin' the grocer's back door!

Crawford Howard

The Diet Drop Out

This slimmin', I thought I had cracked it,
I had lost half a stone, maybe more,
Then we had them oul' bloomin' wet summers,
An' the pounds piled back on by the score.

For sure, what can ye do when it's rainin',
An' on holiday you're meant to be,
Instead of spenin' yer time outside walkin',
Ye'd go into a cafe for tea!

An as you queued up at the counter,
The temptation proved too much for you,
Ye'd grab a cream bun, as you're passin',
Or a slice of Black Forest Gateau!

Then this feelin' of guilt came upon ye,
Ye thought, 'Wan time can't do me much harm,'
Then picked up a few chocolate biscuits,
Tho' your calorie counter'd sounded the alarm.

But as wan bad day followed another,
An' they kept gettin' wetter, an' wetter,
Ye thought, fish an' chips, or hamburgers,
Would perhaps make ye feel a bit better.

The weans were all girnin' an yappin',
For sweeties or ice cream, or Coke,
An' ye sat in the car, an ye ate them,
Though the thought of it now, makes ye boke!

Ye remembered all your good intentions,
Tae get yer body back under control,
But the puddles were fillin' the roadway,
So it put ye off goin' for a stroll.

Now the hand on the scales shows an increase,
An' you're gettin' to the end of your tether,
So if somebody says, 'Boys, you're putting on weight!'
Just blame it all on the bad weather!

Maud Steele

Effects of Age

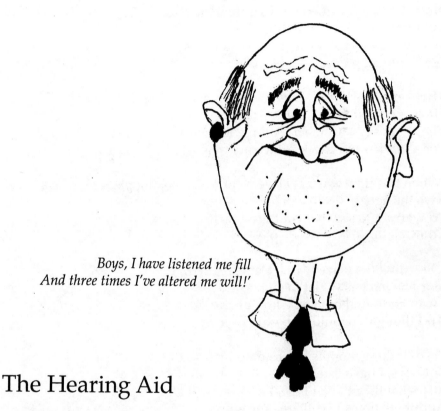

*Boys, I have listened me fill
And three times I've altered me will!'*

The Hearing Aid

Oul' Davie McCann had been deaf many years.
What folk said he never could tell,
Then one day he spotted an advert that claimed
He could once more hear clear as a bell.

And into the bargain, with this, do ye mind,
This chip and transistor machine,
In size, shape and colour was so well designed
That in use it would never be seen.

So Dave kept the advert (he tore it out rough),
Then made an appointment to try,
Well! Lo and behold ye! It worked right enough,
And so he decided to buy.

Now the thing seemed no more than the size of a bug,
Yet he heard all the sounds of the air,
With the gadget stuck in at the back of his lug
And covered forbye with his hair.

Thus now hearing all, Davie went on his way,
Having happily paid up the fee.
The agent says, 'Come back three months from today,
For a service and check, which are free.

'When this time was up, Dave went back, looking pleased.
Says the agent, 'It still works like new.
I'd warrant to say that your lifestyle has eased.
Your relations, I'd say, are pleased too.'

'Oh—divil the plazed,' oul' Davie replied,
'For I haven't as yet let them know.
I wanted to find out just who's on my side,
And thought 'twould be best to lie low!

'So of it these months I've said nothing at all,
But boys, I have listened me fill
Just what they think of me, I now know it all
And three times I've altered me will!'

Billy Ritchie

48

Forty! Who's Countin'

Well, I'm goin' tae be forty the morrow,
And sure forty is not all that oul,
But ye hear some brat callin' ye an oul' doll,
And ye feel ye could knock him out coul'.

But when ye have time tae think o'er it,
Ye can mind what you thought of it still,
That most folk were past it at thirty,
And at forty they were over the hill!

Now it always had been my ambition,
Tae reach forty without a grey hair,
So if one came to my attention,
I'd make sure it did not stay long there.

But I'll relax after the morrow,
And let meself grow old with grace,
For, ye always know ones that's been tintin'
It just doesn't match their oul' face!

And Lord! Not another wee wrinkle!
I never saw that one before,
So I'll buy some of that 'Oil of Ulay'
And hope it prevents any more.

Some people say, 'Don't call them wrinkles,
It's nicer to say "Laughter Lines"'!
If that was what done it, I'm tellin' ye,
I must a had some quare laughs in me time!

Ye might catch a glimpse of your reflection,
In them shop mirrors as ye go through,
And for a second ii just doesn't hit ye,
That thon middle-aged woman, is YOU!

Ye run into some childhood acquaintance,
She may be dressed up in jewels and fur,
But ye spot the grey hairs and you're thinkin'
'Boys! I'm stickin' it better than her!'

While you're sayin' 'Hello, and how are ye?'
And she's saying somethin' the same,
Ye're racking yer brains, but it's useless,
For ye just can't remember her name!

And as ye retreat in confusion,
Ye start thinkin' 'Me memory's gone!
Is this the onset of me dotage?'
Now there's something to ponder upon!

The weans think I'm just an oul' fogey,
They now won't wear one thing that I choose,
Their eyes open wide in pure horror,
Sayin' 'I wouldn't be seen DEAD in them shoes!'

But some people hold other opinions,
They say your life's only begun,
When ye reach that 4, O, you should venture,
To find your own place in the sun.

But, the back's a bit dodgy, the eyes a bit dim,
And of youth I have not found the fountain,
So tomorrow they'll say, 'Are ye forty today?'
I'll say, 'Aye, I'm just forty. Who's countin''

Maud Steele

'Troubles' and War

The Angel of Sandy Row

One Saturday night, I'd been having a jar
And was walking back home from a Sandy Row bar -
I'd had far too many, it wasn't a joke,
So I turned up an entry to have a good boke...
When I lifted my head, I began to feel sicker,
And swore, there and then, that I'd give up the liquor,
For, standing before me, all shiny and bright,
Was a figure that gave me one helluva fright...
He'd great, flowing robes that came down to his ankle -
The likes of him never was seen up the Shankill!
Sez he, "I'm an angel!"... sez I, "You're a what?"
Sez he, "I'm an angel!"... sez I, "That you're not -
If you're really an angel, then where are your wings,
And why aren't you plucking your heavenly strings,
And surely you've got better places to go
Than standing up entries in old Sandy Row?"
Sez he, "Willie, dear, I'm here in disguise,
For I'm one of the Old Boy's heavenly spies
(Though, up there, they think I'm a bit of a laugh,
For my number is double-oh-six and a half!)
He's sent me to Ulster to look at the scene,
And to find out the difference 'twixt Orange and Green,
For we've heard nasty rumours that Satan is grinning,
And that evil and badness in Ulster are winning...!"
Sez I, "Mister, dear, it's the truth that you're speaking,
For the Fenians all over the Province are sneaking -
They're getting in everywhere, Lord, but they're tricky...
You couldn't be up to the games of a Mickey!"
Well, the angel he looked at me hard, for a while,

Then he lifted his head, and he gave a wee smile -
It was like he was laughing at some private joke,
And a feeling of anger in me was awoke.
So I sez, "Listen, Mac - are you Fenian or Prod?"
Sez he, "Willie, dear, I'm the same as my God,
And He doesn't care if you're black, or your white,
If you're Orange or Green, or you're left, or you're right,
If you're family's all Prods, or Fenians, or Yids,
For everyone here is just one of His kids..."
Now, you'll agree that a statement like that was a shocker -
It was clear as a bell he was clean off his rocker...
And he surely knew nothing at all about God
If he thought that a Mick was as good as a Prod!
Was he out on his geg? Was he having a jest?
I decided to put the idea to the test,
So, sez I, "Tell us this - have you heard of King Billy?
Or even the Sash, or the fair Orange Lily?
Do you know of the Blues, or of brave Derry's walls?
Did you know that Old Nick has a house on the Falls?"
Well, he just shook his head, and leaned back on the wall,
So, sez I, "Do you not know your Bible at all?"
Now, I go to my church, like a decent Prod should,
And decided to do the poor fellow some good,
And I said, "Tell you what - I'm taking you home,
And, before you go back, you'll know all about Rome -
When you're up there in Heaven, you'll have lots new to tell...
Like, for instance, the divil speaks Gaelic in Hell!"
Well, in no time at all, we were back at my house,
And there, at the door, was Big Jinny, my spouse,
And the look on her face made me weak at the knees,
So, quick as a flash, sez I, "Jinny, please,
I want you to meet a good buddy of mine -
I don't know his name, but his number'll do fine...
He's one of those spies, like that double-oh-seven...
And, believe it or not, his headquarters is heaven...
He's come for his supper, so get out the pan
And give him a feed that is fit for a man!'
Well, her face was a picture, but, give her due,
She stuck out her hand, and said "How d'you do?

From Heaven to Belfast is many a mile,
So, now that you're here, you must stop for a while!'
One thing about Jinny, she knows how to bake,
And there, on the table she put... ANGEL cake!
Your man was quite pleased (you could tell by his face),
And he said, "Here, I'm glad I came down to this place!'
Well, after the teas we sat down for a chat,
And we talked about this and we talked about that,
And I told him the way things were in Belfast,
And how all the Prods would fight to the last
To maintain our religion the best that we could
The way that our forefathers said that we should,
I told him about my own L.O.L.,
And I showed him my sash (and I wore it as well),
And then I brought out my wee Orange flute
And decided to give it a bit of a toot...
I played him "The Sash", and I played "Dolly's Brae"...
Sez he, "Willie, dear, you fairly can play -
But lend me your flute, and I'll give you an air
That's just a bit different from those you played there!"
So I gave him the flute, and he started to play...
Lord, I'll never forget it till my dying day,
For the notes that he played made us sit there, quite still -
They rose up in the air, the whole house to fill...
They were soft, they were sweet... they brought tears to my eyes...
And I suddenly felt... so old and so wise...
Then a funny thing happened... I tell you no lie...
Your man touched my arm - and I started to FLY...
With him at my side, I rose in the air,
And out of the house, over Shaftesbury Square -
I was so bloomin' scared that I started to shiver,
And my arms and my legs were all of a quiver
As the two of us kept floating on through the night,
Passing the old City Hall on the right,
And there was the shipyard, the Dufferin Dock,
The Liverpool boat, and the grand Albert Clock,
And there were the people, the girls and the boys,
And the lights of the city, the smell and the noise,
The hooting of horns... and also, of course,

The police and the army were down there in force -
We stepped up the pace, and began to fly faster...
Lord, meeting your man was a downright disaster!
We soared up the Falls, towards Andersonstown...
And that's where we stopped... I had a look down...
The rooves of the houses were sort of transparent -
The reason, to me, was not too apparent,
But one little house I especially spied...
I could see right into the bedroom inside -
You could tell, at a glance, where THEIR loyalties lay,
For the Pope on the wall gave their leanings away!
And there was a man, on a wee wicker chair,
With a frown on his face, and a sad hopeless stare..
And a woman was there at the foot of the bed...
When I looked further up my heart turned to lead -
When I saw what was there, I just couldn't help crying,
For there, on that bed, a youngster lay, dying -
And the funny thing was, when I saw it was sick,
It just didn't matter that it was a Mick...
Those Fenians might breed families of nine,
But that child could easily have been one of mine,
And its father could easily have been my own brother -
Sure, the Prods and the Micks were just like each other...
Now, whether or not, 'twas because of the drink,
For the first time in ages, I started to think,
And I found I was telling myself to act wise,
And to look all around me, and open my eyes...
Now, all of the time I was watching that room,
His nibs on the flute was still playing that tune -
He handled the instrument just like a master...
Then, all of a sudden the tempo got faster
And we started to move away from Belfast,
Away from the present, and back to the past...
The music, it brought me right back to my youth,
To the first girl I loved, my darling wee Ruth...
I could see her again, her eyes, and her smile...
I could see us again, at the wee country stile...
And remembered the way that our families turned odd,
For she was a Mick... and I was a Prod...

I saw it again, the night Ruthie died,
And the way that her family kept me outside...
I remembered all this, and felt so... so sad,
For MY folks turned out to be just as bad -
They told me to marry into my own,
Instead of a girl whose allegiance was Rome -
And, remembering this, I knew very well
There were Prods as well as Mickies in Hell!
I remembered, as well, that God sent His Son
To say "Love Your Neighbour" and he meant EVERY one...
And while I remembered, the music played on...
Then it stopped... I looked up... the angel was... gone...
Well, the next thing I knew, I woke up in my bed
With a mouth like a sewer, and a bomb in my head,
And Jinny was lying there, tonguing and screaming...
Everything normal! I must have been dreaming!
But that dream was a dream that filled me with shame,
And, from that day to this, I've not been the same,
For the music I heard lingers on in my mind,
And I swear that I'll never again be so blind -
Till the day that I die, I'll treat all men the same...
Even the ones with a Catholic name!
And, if God thinks I'm worth it, He'll take me to Heaven
And make me a spy... maybe double-oh-seven?
And then, perhaps, some day, if you're up Sandy Row,
And up a wee entry you might have to go,
Who knows? You might see me, in a shiny white suit,
And there, in my hand, my wee Orange flute...
And, if you ask me, real nice, I might play you that tune...
But, for now, I'm away... sure, I'll see you... real soon...

Bill Nesbitt

Song of Belfast

(This poem may be sung to the air: 'Song of the Clyde')

I'll sing you a song of the town of Belfast,
Where the oul' Union Jack is still nailed to the mast,
But the flag-pole is shaking with every blast
Oh! a wonderful town is the town of Belfast.
We've wonderful factories and shipyards as well
So to keep up employment we'll blow them to Hell
For in bullets and bombs the resources are vast
And the bullet and bomb sing the song of Belfast

Chorus:
Poor oul' Belfast—how long can it last
For there's bits disappearing with every blast
It may have no future but boy! what a past,
A wonderful town is the song of Belfast.

Now in Belfast there's more than the weasel goes 'pop'
For there's smashing reductions in every shop.
I know a wee lad took his girl to a ball
They went in through the door and came out through the wall!
It's not even safe to go into a pub
For the bits of glass flying would slice off yer gub.
I went out last night for a couple of beers
And bejasus! the lounge bar came down round my ears!

And there was little Willie who to please King Billy hit a poor oul'
    Mickey on the head.
There was little Seamus—he will soon be famous—he blew up a van
    of Ormo bread,
There was Sean and Michael on a motor cycle flying up and down
    the Springfield Road
And they're throwing boulders at the British soldiers who are only
    doing what they are told.

There was Bernadette—I'm sure she's talkin' yet—I seen her on the
    Telly-V
And by all the powers they went on for hours and hours by courtesy
    of B.B.C.
There was all the talkers minus Brian Faulkner like big Ian P. and
    Gerry Fitt
But I know a fellow who was watching 'tele' said they talked an
    awful lot of rubbish.

Chorus

Now the poor starving masses all stand in a daze
When they hear of the things that go on in the Maze,
For the fellas in there don't like eating at all,
For they keep throwin' their dinners out over the wall.
Now the doctor's say walking is good for your health
But bejasus! it's not like you walk on the '12th'
And if you get lifted—what a terrible fate!
You get sent up the Crumlin until ye escape!

Crawford Howard

The Breadman

(This poem may be sung to the air: 'Jesse James')

Willie Thompson was a man who drove an Ormo van.
He sold the best of bread.
He didn't make much money but this wasn't very funny
For the wife could never get him out of bed.

Chorus
Now poor Willie's dead and gone
But his fame still lingers on.
He drove the fastest breadvan in Belfast
And he had three mighty sons all brought up on Paris buns
And they'll all be driving breadvans till the last.

Through flame and shot and shell Willie drove his breadvan well.
He didn't give a damn for the I.R.A.
Till one morning up the 'Falls' he was whistling 'Derry's Walls'
And they swore they'd drive his poor old van away.
Willie jumped down from the van and a battle soon began.
Vienna rolls and 'crusties' he did fling
And amidst the flying bread, where men lay cold and dead
They stood amazed to hear old Willie sing:

'With a gun, with a gun
Ah ye can't get a van with a gun!
You can take yer oul' revolver And shove it over the Border
But you can't get a van with a gun!'

Now many a man lay dead with a pan loaf through his head
Or murdered by a flying Paris bun.
There was very few would dare to face a flying current square
And the I.R.A. were falling one by one,
Then a sharp Vienna roll it took its deadly toll
And Willie lay spreadeagled on the ground
And the poor old van was made into a barricade
And the spent pan loaves was lyin' all around.

Chorus

When the nights are cold and dark, where the Ormo bread-vans park
They say that Willie's presence you can feel.
You can hear his eerie calls as he sets off for the Falls,
In a ghostly van with Willie at the wheel,
And the British Army say, as they fight the I.R.A.
Old Willie's ghost is worth a thousand men,
For the Provos all keep clear and the Officials shake with fear
When they hear that Willie Thompson rides again
And on that final morn when old Gabriel blows his horn
To rouse the mighty company of the dead.
If you see an Ormo van and St. Peter's buying a 'pan'
It's only Willie Thompson selling bread!

Crawford Howard

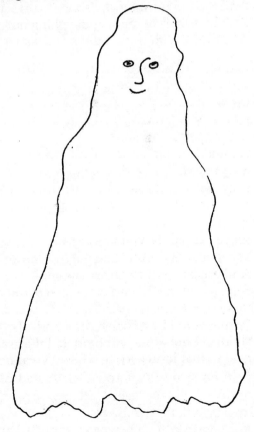

My Mother's Shawl

The sky was dark and when prayers were said,
My mother happed us up in bed,
My father was working across the sea,
And we'd prayed to God that safe he'd be.

The sky was red and sparks were flying,
When I woke to the sound of my mother crying,
My brothers and sisters were crying as well,
And I thought I had wakened up somewhere in Hell.

There were loud banging noises all over the place,
And the red burning sky shone on everyone's face,
People were screaming and yelling outside
And along with my brothers and sisters, I cried.

The floor of the bedroom was glistening red,
Where reflecting splinters of glass lay spread,
My mother 'tween crying and saying her prayers,
Led us to safety, under the stairs.

With her shawl wrapped around us, she held us close to her,
And I felt fear and strong love go trembling through her,
With each loud explosion, she drew us all tight,
And prayed, "Sacred Heart, please protect us this night."

We sat in the darkness, weeping and groaning,
My mother's arms round us, rocking and moaning,
And the hot burning tears she shed with each moan,
Fell on our cheeks and were mixed with our own.

Then one loud explosion drowned all other sound,
Shook all the walls and trembled the ground,
And in that loud silence, I knew I was dreaming,
As it seemed from a distance, my mother was screaming.

She hurried us out as the house kept shaking,
And under my bare feet, I felt the floor quaking,
She opened the hall door and there she did stand,
Pleading for someone to give her a hand.

We all stood behind her, gripping her skirt,
Shivering with fear and covered with dirt,
But oh, how I wished she would close the hall door,
And return to the darkness and safety once more.

For the scene in that street where I loved to play,
Is etched in my memory 'til my dying day,
A cauldron of strangers were swirling around,
Where planks, bricks and slates lay all over the ground.

Sharp piercing whistles rained down through the air,
As the people crouched low with a loud wailing prayer,
And every explosion brought forth a hot gust,
Of black blinding smoke and dry choking dust.

A deep throbbing noise from the sky overhead,
Filled me with wonder, with fear, and with dread,
And it seemed that this mad world, while passing us by,
Had turned a deaf ear to my poor mother's cry.

Despairing of help, she closed the hall door,
And guided us back to the coal-hole once more,
Where all that long night, which seemed like a year,
We sat 'til she whimpered, "Thank God... the all-clear."

With her shawl still around us, she sighed with relief,
And the tears that she shed now were not tears of grief,
She hugged us, she kissed us, she wept with delight,
And thanked God for helping her all through that night.

Then out to the kitchen we scrambled once more,
Where the ceiling and black soot covered the floor,
We washed and got dressed as best as we could,
And went round to the school for hot tea and food.

On my way to the school I got quite a fright,
At the place where I'd played that previous night,
Where a woman had chased us away from her door,
There was now only rubble... there were houses no more.

Later that day, amidst panic and fuss,
With clothes tied in bundles, we boarded a bus,
Where we all sat in silence, bewildered and dazed,
And passed along streets where houses still blazed.

The streets became roads I had ne'r before seen,
Flanked by hedges and square fields of green,
We were brought to a farmhouse as a new night was falling,
And I listened in awe to different birds calling.

Weary and tired we went in through the door,
And stood on a big broad flag-stoned floor.
In amazement I gazed at a fire by the wall,
That had neither fender, nor grating at all.

From the ceiling two oil lamps gave off a soft light,
And the scene was so peaceful it put fear to flight,
With the sweet scent of turf smoke I'd not smelt before,
I closed my eyes slowly and saw nothing more.

Well, we stayed in the country for almost a year,
Away from the bombs and free from all fear,
Where I learned to make butter and helped to make hay,
And discovered new things about life every day.

One time coming home from school through the fields,
I noticed a hen with her chicks at her heels,
She saw me and spread out her wings like a hood,
Then wrapped them around her poor frightened brood.

No author can write, nor orator speak,
Of the love mothers have for the young and the weak,
As I looked at that hen, I could nought but recall,
That night I had sheltered 'neath my mother's shawl.

Seamus Lavery

Gardening

The Garden

Would you look at my dahlias, they're failures,
    and the greenfly has flummoxed my phlox.
My sunflowers stoop, my delphiniums droop,
    and something has savaged my stocks.
My willow tree's wilted and terribly tilted,
    I've made a right ass of my asters,
And though it seems crazy, even my daisies
    turn out to be downright disasters.

My anemones have their own enemies,
    my begonias are so woe-begone,
There's ants in my poor anthirrhinums,
    and masses of moss in my lawn.
My sweet peas are sour, my lobelias won't flower,
    my cornflowers suffer from bunions
And my radishes rot, my rose has black spot
    and my sage bushes don't know their onions!

I tried some chrysanths, but they're terrible plants,
    I can't seem to grow them at all.
My artichoke's croaked (by chickweed choked),
    and my wallflower's gone to the wall.
My peas haven't flowered, for they've all been devoured
    by some insect that fancies their taste,
And some little hallions have ruined my scallions,
    the whole thing's a terrible waste!

It's really too bad to see just how sad
    are the hearts of my poor gladioli.
My thyme is too tardy, and not very hardy,
    and my Honesty looks most unholy.
My runner bean's walked, and my broad beans have baulked,
    my cucumber has lost all its cool,
And my marrow's no bone, and I grumble and groan
    at the hundreds of weeds I've to pull.

My lupin's in loops, the leaves curled in hoops,
    my nasturtium's nasty to view
My savoys have all sagged, and my leeks all need lagged,
    and my daffodils don't seem to do.
My marigold's dead, for it's more mari-lead,
    as a flower it hadn't much mettle,
And my blackcurrant's bare.... and I'm going to swear,
    for I've gone and been stung by a nettle.

My beetroot are beaten, won't ever be eaten,
    my apples would give you the pip.
My Love-in-a Mist will never be kissed,
    my tulips all give me the slip.
The whole thing's a mess, and the answer, I guess,
    is to know I'm completely defeated,
And to buy some cement, for my urgent intent
    is to have the whole shambles concreted!

Bill Nesbitt

Come into the Garden Fred

Come into the garden Fred.
Look at my plants, they are dead.
Look at my asters,
They're bloomin' disasters
And the weeds grow over my head.

Come into the garden John.
Look what the slugs have done.
They've eaten my beet,
My daisies, my wheat.
I'll murder them from now on.

Come into the garden Fred

Come into the garden Maisie
And see what's been done til my daisy.
It's covered in holes,
'Tho there aren't any moles
It's enough to drive us all crazy.

Come into the garden Stephanie
And look at the fate of my Daphne.
It's leaves are all brown
From the root to the grown,
It looks as if I don't have any.

Come into the garden Bill,
I've just had a awful thrill!
I've looked at my phlox,
It's dead, so're my stocks,
I wish I knew what to kill.

Come into the garden Mary,
My cabbages are really contrary,
They're covered in bugs
And beetles and slugs.
They're not fit to feed my canary.

Come into the garden friend,
I feel I've come to the end
Of digging and weeding
And planting and seeding.
I'll give up less I go round the bend.

Doreen McBride

Family Life

Washday Wonder

Well I'm hanged if I know where they go to,
But disappear they surely do,
Every time that I'm doin' the washin'
I hae one, an' there ought to be two!

Do you think they dissolve in the water?
I just cannot know where they have gone,
When I hoke them out after I've washed them,
Instead of each pair, I hae one!

An' it isn't just once in a wonder,
But the same oul' thing week after week,
D'ye know it's just drivin' me crazy,
Them socks, playing hide an' go seek.

Every time that I look in the basket,
There seems to be more and still more,
An' not even two of them matches,
Wud it not nearly make yer head sore!

By now I have quite a collection
Of socks every colour an' creed
D'ye think when ye put them together,
Is it possible, single socks BREED?

Maud Steele

I scoul, complain an' girn
until I'm scunnered

Do It Yersel'

Wud you credit that some folk could be so handless,
Seems the only one CAN do some jobs is YOU,
I mean simple things that wouldn't take an expert,
Like fittin' on a new roll in the loo!

But naw, ye'll find it sittin, on the cistern,
Or rollin' round the floor among yer feet,
When it really wouldn't take a powerful effort,
To fit it, without gettin' off yer seat!

I scoul, complain an' girn until I'm scunnered,
But I might as well keep quate, not waste me time,
For when that roll gets right down tae the cardboard,
Ye can guess whose hands'll change it, they'll be MINE

Maud Steele

Rest in Peace

(Some chance!)

I woke up wi' a cough an' a splutter,
And this terrible ache in me head,
I staggered across to the bathroom,
Then decided I'd go back to bed.

'I don't think I'll get up this mornin','
I groaned, 'I have got a right dose.'
'Just lie there,' says James, 'I'll go down now,
And make a wee cup o' tay an' some toast.'

'O.K.', I said, 'Just get the weans up.'
An' lay back in bed wi' a sigh,
The next thing I heard a voice shoutin'
'Hi Mammy, did you see my tie?'

I said, 'Naw, did ye look in yer bedroom?'
He says, 'Aye, but I don't see it there,'
So I trailed out o' bed and looked for it,
An' pulled it out from the back of a chair.

I had just settled down when the phone rang,
And nobody seemed to hear it but me,
An' no wonder, for sure ye'd hear nothin'
For the noise blarin' from the T.V.

But still that oul' phone kept on ringin',
'till I just couldn't stand any more,
So I struggled up, goin' to answer it,
And it stopped as me feet touched the floor.

I'd just snuggled back under the blankets,
When another head popped round the door,
She said, 'Mammy, I need dinner money.'
So I put me feet back on the floor.

An' I hoked in me purse for the money,
Then lay back to rest me poor head,
When the weest boy climbed out of his cot,
Sayin' 'Mammy, I'll sleep in your bed!'

So he jumped in and tramped on me stomach,
Then poked at me eyes, pulled me hair,
Then he started to kick off the bedclothes,
'till he nearly drove me to despair.

Then below, I heard not such sweet music,
The recorder! Boys that thing's a curse!
If ye have a sore head, a recorder,
Being played, makes it feel ten times worse!

So at last I just gave up the struggle,
And went down in me oul' dressing gown,
Says James, 'Are ye feelin' a bit better?
Sure I didn't expect you to come down!'

'Feelin' better?' I snapped, 'Glad ye think so!'
An' I near ate the face of me spouse,
'Y'ed get more peace to sleep at the Diamond,
Than ye'd get to rest here in this house!'

Maud Steele

Knock, Knock! Who's There?

I was just home from work, an' the house was a mess,
When who comes to the back door? Oh you'll never guess,
The Reverend Thingmajig, new to the town
An' wan of the elders thought they would – call round!

I don't know what I said as they came through the door,
For me eyes kep' on strayin' tae the mess round the floor,
I felt that embarrassed, as I looked at me feet,
For I'm tellin' you my kitchen was far from bein' neat!

The sink, full of dishes, an' clothes on the chairs,
Books an' toys by the dozen, an' shoes! three or four pair!
They said, 'We were passing and thought we'd drop in,'
But what I was thinkin' was surely a sin!
(I haven't a thing in the house, if they stay,
Oh! what will I do if I have to make tay?)

They said, 'We're in a hurry.' an' of that I was glad,
For a seat to sit down on just couldn't be had,
They hoped they would see me at church the next week,
An' I felt that affronted, I hardly could speak!

If ye had the house shinin', an' as neat as a pin,
Ye could bet yer last penny, not wan soul would come in.
So if you're feelin' lonely, an' company ye'd like,
Then take my advice, just bring in an oul' bike,
Three or four newspapers, toys by the score,
An' scatter them liberally, all roun' the floor,
Forget about hooverin', leave the dishes undone,
An' I'll guarantee ye, dozens of people will come!

Maud Steele

The Orange and the Green

The Rebel Record-player

Wee Willie John McFadyean was a loyal Orange 'Prod,
And he thought that Ian Paisley was just one step down from God.
He thought they ate the 'childer' in the backwoods of Ardoyne,
And he knew that history started with the Battle of the Boyne!

One night he took a brick in his hand and he wandered up the 'Falls'.
He was muttering 'Up the Rangers!' and humming 'Derry's Walls!'
He bust a big shop window, to annoy the Pope of Rome
And he took a record player out and then he staggered home.

Next night they held a 'hooley' in the local Orange Hall
And Willie took his player to make music at the ball.
He chose a stack of records of a very loyal kind,
But when the music started up he nearly lost his mind!

For the Fenian record-player was a rebel to the core,
It played the tunes that Orange Hall had never heard before.
For 'Derry's Walls' and 'Dolly's Brae' it didn't care a fig,
And it speeded up 'God Save The Queen' till it sounded like a jig!

It played the 'Boys of Wexford' and 'The Wearing of the Green'.
Such turmoil in an Orange Hall has never yet been seen.
It played the 'Woods of Upton' and 'The Men of '98,
But when it played 'The Soldier's Song' it sealed wee Willie's fate.

For the boys went clean demented—to the ground wee Will was
    thrown,
And they kicked his ribs in one by one to the tune of 'Garryowen'.
They threw him out the window to a 'Song of Old Sinn Fein',
And they kicked him all down Sandy Row to 'A Nation Once Again!'

The rebel record player was heard no never more,
For they prodded it with deacon poles and threw it on the floor,
But yet it was not finished, 'twas the funniest thing you've seen,
For the flashes flying out of it was orange, white and green.

Wee Willie's up in Purdysburn—he's crazy as a coot,
He just sits there in his padded cell and tootles on his flute,
And when he tries to play 'The Sash' he always gets it wrong,
For halfway through he always finds he's playing 'The Soldier's
    Song'.

There's a moral to this story—what it is I cannot say,
It may be just the ancient one that crime will never pay.
If you ask wee Will McFadyean he says, 'Ah, crime be blowed!'
'If you want to pinch a record-player do it up the Shankill Road!'

Crawford Howard

Paddy's Prayer

Paddy was a Catholic and a man of simple ways
With a Faith that seemed to carry him through life,
Emphatically believing that he who stops and prays,
Would get his needs in times of pressing strife.

When at one time Pat's affairs got something out of hand.
You may find his course of action rather odd,
But he wanted to put through a plea with no hint of demand
And so he wrote a letter straight to God.

'Dear Father, up in Heaven, you will know my need is dire,
So I trust on my request you will not frown,
But I work out at the moment that the least I do require
And appeal to You to grant us fifty 'pound'.

'Then he popped it in the postbox thinking, 'He will find a way.
'On the envelope he simply wrote 'To God.'
In the due course it was lifted by the middle of next day
By the postman, Billy Mac., who was a Prod.!

Now Billy bein' a member of the local Orange Lodge
Brought the matter to a meeting for to press.
'If our hearts are set in charity, let's not the issue dodge,
Can't we help Paddy in his dark distress?'

'For although he is a Catholic, he's still a decent lad,
I'm sure you all know him as well as I.
If we can't make an effort, then I'd say it's rather sad
And though funds are low, it's only right to try!

Well the matter was debated and got nearly shelved away
While charity with funding had to strive,
Until it was decided by all present there that day
That the best that they could do was 'twenty five'.

So the cash was sent to Paddy with a note to wish him well,
On the headed paper of the orange and blue,
Expressing their desiring of his worries for to quell
And hoping that perhaps 'twould see him through.

As Pat strolled on the roadway in a further seven days,
He met Seamus, whom he'd told about his plan.
'Just how has it been going?' with a twinkle Seamus says,
'How'd you get on with your letter till Yer Man?'

'Did you get help like you asked for in answer to your 'prayer?'
'Says Pat, 'I knew He'd help me if He could
For He always has responded to a justified affair
And He sent help to me like I knew He would.'

'Still His wisdom I now question and my faith begins to fall
And with me you'll know for certain that's no laugh,
For He sent it through the brethern of the local Orange Hall,
And would you believe? The buggers kept the half!'

Billy Ritchie

The Wee Tin Flute

I'm driven till distraction, I don't know what to do…
I've hunted for it everywhere, I'm in an awful stew –
I'm sorta lost without it, for it really was a beaut…
So please, please, won't ye tell me – have ye seen my wee tin flute?

I've lukked up in the attic, and underneath the stair,
I've hunted through the parlour, I've lukked just everywhere –
I've rummaged through the sideboord, and on the kitchen shelf…
Whatever am I goin' till do, for the morra is the Twelfth!

Now, I go with Lily Johnston, on me she has a crush,
But if I haven't got my wee tin flute, I'll surely get the push,
For what's the point of coortin' her, sure, I'd luk awful silly,
For a man without a wee tin flute is no good to thon Lily!

Ach, can't ye jist imagine me out walkin' with the band –
I'd luk an awful Charley without m'wee flute in my hand…
For years, I've tuk it till the field, ye cud hear the girls all shout
And go intil hysterics when I pulled my wee flute out!

The one I think last saw it was the girl nixt dure, Big Nelly –
She reckoned, when she saw it, that it should be on the telly…
And the girls at work all loved it, they'd niver seen the like –
I'd better find it very soon, or they'll all go out on strike!

Ach, I miss it awful badly, what am I goin' till do?
Most of it is orange, but the tip is coloured blue –
Thon flute and me together have come through thick and thin…
So, if ye find it, hand it back – you don't know where it's bin…!

Now, I can't do without it, though to you it's not much use,
For one end's sorta twisty, and the other's comin' loose –
My oul' man bought it for me, with joy his eyes did shine…
Sez he, "I'm very proud, wee son – your wee flute's jist like mine!"

I tuk it till a music class, that was fairly racent,
But the teacher made me put it back, for she said it wasn't dacent...
And I played with it till picture queues when I was nearly skint –
I didn't make much money... but I got my name in print!

I mind, when I was just thirteen, the vicar came til call –
My oul' boy didn't like him, he liked him not at all...
He didn't drink, or smoke, or swear, the man was such a bore –
So I just pulled out my wee tin flute, and he bolted for the door!

Some men can chat the weemin up with words as sweet as honey,
And some can git just anywhere by flashin' aff their money,
But my way's sorta different, it works a perfect charm –
I jist give a toot on my wee tin flute before I chance my arm!

A man can't go on livin', when his wee tin flute is... gone...

Three years ago, I tuk real bad, I went intil the City,
And the doctors lukked at my wee flute, sez they, "That's awful
    pretty!"
And the specialists examined it, it caused a great sensation –
But they niver got my wee tin flute, in spite of the operation!

I met a girl at a disco dance, she said her name was Nancy –
She really was a smasher, and till her, I tuk a fancy –
I ast her cud I take her home… we had till get a taxi…
And she felt my flute, and sez, "That's cute – it makes me hellish
    sexy!"

Ach, I feel undressed without it, I really do feel bare,
And I don't know how I'll manage, for I haven't got a spare…
So, if there's anyone you know who happens till have two,
Ast him wud he len' us one – I'll keep it good as new!

I've lukked in all the bedrooms, and in the bathroom, too,
For I often had a toot on it when visitin' the loo…
It isn't very hard till miss, for it measures near a foot –
So please, please, won't ye tell me – have ye seen my wee tin flute?

I'm feelin' most unhappy, and life is awful flat –
Things haven't felt the same at all since I lost my you-know-what…
Only one thing left till do – I'll shoot myself at dawn…
For a man can't go on livin', when his wee tin flute is… gone…

Bill Nesbitt

A Drop of the Craiter

Feeling Fragile

I'm feelin' sort of fragile, and far from hale and hearty.
I must have had a smashin' time at Willie Wilson's party!
I can't mind much about it, but I must have had a ball,
For the fact is, at the moment, I don't feel good at all!

I've a sneakin' recollection of seeing Jinny Jones,
And I've got a sinkin' feelin' right down inside my bones
That I wasn't quite as sensible as might have been supposed
For, though I just can't stand her, I've a feelin' I proposed!'

The trouble is, I can't think straight, for I had a right old sup,
And boys, I'm awful worried that she went and took me up!
I just can't mind her answer, and I don't know what to do,
But one thing's sure and certain, I'm in a fair old stew.

I know I ought to phone her, but I'd get an awful fright
If I discovered what I'm fearing turns out to be right!
I cannot even write to her, for then without a doubt,
If she had it down on paper, I could never wriggle out!

Didn't I? Or did I? The answer's got me vexed.
Small wonder that I'm lookin' green, and feelin' fierce perplexed!
Have I gone and stuck my silly head inside a bridal halter?
Are my days of freedom numbered? Am I headed for the altar?

What did Jinny answer me, all those hours ago?
Oh, boys, I'd be delighted if I thought that she'd said "No!"
Just think, a drop of porter has led to my undoin',
And a glass or two of whiskey has brought me near to ruin!

Here, wait a minute... there's the phone! "Hello?... Yes, this is me."
"Oh!... Jinny.... it's yourself... well, no... I'm not exactly free...
"You want to ask a question? Well... all right... go ahead...
I'm dreading it, but - hold on, Jinny… what was that you said…?"

"You say you're feelin' fierce ashamed at what you did last night?
"You had a drop too much to drink, and passed out like a light?
"You cannot mind the things you said? And now you want to
    know...?
"I'm sorry! I've forgotten too... So Jinny, cheerio!"

Bill Nesbitt

I'm feelin' sort of fragile

The Drunken Lad

Wee Will got a sampling of whiskey
And ended up drunk as a fool.
He was found hanging on to the railings
Encircling the Primary School.

Around him a crowd quickly gathered.
Some offered to lend him a hand,
But trying to make him walk homewards,
Was useless, he just couldn't stand.

This attracted two policemen's attention,
Who said, 'We'll take care of this lad.'
They bundled him in the patrol car
To chauffeur him back to his pad.

They were met at the door by his mother,
Who yelled, 'Disobedient wee BRAT!
You were told to be home here by tea-time,
So to learn you, just take that and that!'

Then she hammered him round by the table,
With a left after right round the lugs,
Till a swipe that went wild hit the dresser
And brought down a plate and two mugs.

'Now look what has happened!' she guldered,
'Of that broken delf you're the cause.
If you give me an ounce more of bother
I'll take it and wallop your jaws!'

'So sit down on that chair in the corner,
And be quiet, with no if or but,
For you're shaping to be like your father,
And he was a drunken wee scut!'

'And another thing—wasting your money,
You'd squander it all so you would.
If your hangover's bad in the morning
May the devil of it give you good!'

At that she left off the barging
And back to the policemen she strolled.
'I think that will sort out the matter,
At times lads must be well controlled!'

The policemen just gaped in amazement,
But later they giggled with glee,
For the 'lad' was a wee man of sixty,
And his mother a spritely ninety-three!

Billy Ritchie

Violetta

(This poem may be sung to the air: 'Johnny Lad')

Once there was an oul' doll who worked down in the 'Co',
Her name was—Violetta—and she came from Sandy Row.
Singing, 'Oh would ye go and are ye comin' out?
I'll buy ye fifty tatie farls and half a pint of stout!'

Her husband was an oul' lad who worked down in the yard.
There was not a pub in Belfast from which he was not barred.
Singing, 'Oh would ye go and are ye comin' out?
I'll buy ye fifty tatie farls and half a pint of stout!'

And every Friday evening wherever he chanced to roam,
You'd hear him singing this oul' song as he came rolling home,
'Hear my song, Violetta, hear my song beneath the moon
Put the pan on, Violetta, for I will be home soon!'

Now Violetta's temper was gettin' more ferocious,
For she was always sober and he was always stocious,
Singing, 'Oh would ye go and are ye comin' out?
I'll buy ye fifty tatie farls and half a pint of stout!'

So one night in a temper she kicked him out of bed.
She grabbed the bloody frying pan and bate him round the head.
Singing, 'Oh would ye go and are ye comin' out
I'll buy ye fifty tatie farls and half a pint of stout!'

Then she grabbed the bottle of whiskey and put it 'till her head
And danced around the kitchen singing fit to wake the dead,
Singing, 'Oh would ye go an' are ye comin' out
I'll buy ye fifty tatie farls and half a pint of stout!'

Then she found she liked the taste of it as she poured it down her throttle,
So she ran down 'till the corner pub and brought another bottle,
Singing, 'Oh would ye go and are ye comin' out?
I'll buy ye fifty tatie farls and half a pint of stout!'

Now the moral of this story, it really can't be missed
For the oul' lad's always sober now and she is always drunk
Singing, 'Oh would ye go and are ye comin' out?
I'll buy ye fifty tatie farls and half a pint of stout!
Singing, 'Oh would ye go and are ye comin' out?
I'll buy ye fifty tatie farls and half a pint of stout!'

Crawford Howard

*Then she found she liked the taste of it
as she poured it down her throttle*

Love of Home

My Wee House

It was only a wee house, as wee houses go,
Two rooms upstairs and two down below,
With the dur always open and no thought of danger,
But a warm hearty welcome for friend and for stranger.

Though it was only oil cloth that covered the flur,
It was always kept clean, aye , clean to be sure,
With a big wooden table I'd scrubbed almost white,
And a black-leaded hearth, with fire burning bright.

It was not always tidy and not always neat,
When the childer played games on the flur at m'feet,
But at least they were happy, as happy cud be,
And that was the main thing that mattered to me.

It had no central heating, yet always was warm,
And it kept us all safe through manys a storm,
And on coul winter nights, round the fire we wud sit,
While the childer toul stories, I'd listen and knit.

On Saturday nights, with the wee ones all in,
I'd bring in the big bath, made out of tin,
When I had them all washed, and safely in bed,
I wud sit on the sofa, and shower m'poor head.

I didn't have much, and what I had was soon gone,
But sure if I ran short there was always the pawn,
When the shoes and the clothes that we wore every Sunday,
Were cleaned and wrapped up for me Uncle's on Monday.

Aye, them was the days that they say was hard,
When to go to the toilet, y'went to the yard,
And y'sat w'yer feet lifted aff the flur,
When the rain or the snow blew in under the dur.

Ah but many's the day when the sun wud shine,
We wud go on a tram to the end of the line,
Where I'd sit on m'shawl, and think it was grand,
As m'childer played games on the Greencastle sand.

And on warm summer evenings, I wud git m'wee stool,
And I'd sit at the dur with m'needles and wool,
Sometimes I wud knit and other times darn,
While me and wee Cassie wud have a quare yarn.

Then things started changin', for better or worse,
And some o'them changes t'me was a curse,
For the gas was tuk out, and electric put in,
And the bills I'd t'pay then, was really a sin.

And with T.V.s and such things I was near driv mad,
For m'childer just wanted what all their friends had,
And I knew that t'plase them, I wud always be poor,
For the tick-men were nivir away from m'dur.

Well, the years rolled by, and with m'childer all grown,
And all of them married, w'homes of their own,
I thought I'd have pace, there bein' just him and me,
But oh dear no, this was not to be.

For a lock o'months back, this letter did come,
Which said my wee house was only a slum,
My lovely wee house, that knowed sweet times and bitter,
Was now called a slum, by some City Hall scitter.

Well I nearly dropped dead where I stud on the flur,
When in comes wee Cassie, m'neighbour next dur,
The colour of death, and I wasn't much better,
And she had in her hand, the very same letter.

The rest of m'neighbours had got letters too,
And it seemed there was nothing at all we cud do,
We had protest marches all over the place,
And we argued until we were blue in the face.

But them City Hall ones are a very tough foe,
And the end of it all was, we just had to go,
And the day I was lavin', I lingered a while,
Just to be with the friends I had knowed from a chil'.

When I redd out m'wee house, m'heart was real sore,
And I thought m'house sensed, I'd be back there no more,
For the dur gave a screech, and the windys all shook,
As I stud on the futpath, t'have my last look.

Well, they putt him an' me in a high rise flat,
With people on this side, and people on that,
With people above us and people below,
But not one friendly face in that place did I know.

In my own wee house I cud always luk out,
And see the wee childer all playin' about,
An' take m'wee stool, and sit at the dur,
But in this flat I cud just see the sky and the flur.

Then one day last week I went out for a dander,
And they say where the heart lies, the feet always wander,
I walked to the street where I'd lived all my life,
First as a child and then as a wife.

When I saw my wee house, I just stud there and cried,
I felt coul all over, and empty inside,
My house, that had sheltered my family and me,
Was stripped bare and naked, for all eyes to see.

The hall dur was lyin' down flat on the flur,
And the kitchen was covered with plaster and stur,
The slates were all gone, and the rafters as well,
And my lovely wee house was now just a shell.

Then down the street came this great big crane,
With a big iron ball on a long heavy chain,
It stopped just fernenst me, and then swung round,
And my poor helpless house was brought to the ground.

I opened my mouth, but I just cudn't spake,
And I had the same feelin' y'get at a wake,
A lifetime of caring, had just come to an end,
And I'd just seen the death of a very dear friend.

For my house was a home, a home full of life,
A haven of love, in a world full of strife,
A place of comfort, a refuge from pain,
And now it was gone, with one swing of a crane.

I turned on m'heel, and m'legs were shakin'
I walked slowly away, with a heart that was breakin'
I went towards that flat, with a feelin' of dread,
And I wished, like my wee house, I wished I was dead.

Seamus Lavery

The Only Place For Me

I'll speak to you of Belfast, stranger, if you want to know,
So listen, and I'll tell you why I love this city so.

BELFAST... is an Ulsterman, with features dour and grim,
It's a pint of creamy porter, it's a Sunday morning hymn,
A steaming pasty supper, or vinegar with peas,
A homely little cafe where they serve you farmhouse teas,
A banner on July the Twelfth, a sticky toffee apple,
A righteous little Gospel Hall, a Roman Catholic chapel,
A "Tele' boy with dirty face, a slice of apple tart,
A fry upon a Saturday, hot coal brick, on a cart,
A Corporation gas-man, complete with bowler hat,
A wee shop on a corner with a friendly bit of chat,
An old man in a duncher, a woman in a shawl,
A pinch of snuff, a tatie farl, a loyal Orange Hall,
A tobacco smell in York Street, a bag of yellow man,
An Easter egg what's dyed in whin, a slice of Ormo pan,
A youngster with some sprickly-begs inside a wee jam-jar,
A meeting at the Customs House, an old Victorian bar,
Mud banks on the Lagan when the tide is running low,
A man collecting "refuse", bonfires in Sandy Row,
A bag of salty dullis, a bowl of Irish stew,
Goldfish down in Gresham Street, a preacher in a queue,
A portrait of King Billy upon a gable wall,
A flower seller on a stool outside the City Hall,
A half moon round a doorstep, a "polisman" on guard,
A pedlar crying "Deplh for regs!", a little whitewashed yard.

And there's your answer, stranger, and now I'm sure you'll see
Why Belfast is the only place in all the world for me.

Bill Nesbitt

The Supernatural

The 'Prod' Poltergeist

There is a place in East Belfast, in the place they call the 'Hack'.
(That's short for Ballyhackamore in case you're losin' track).
It belongs to some good Catholic folks called Sean and Bernadette
They bought it twenty years ago and they're livin' in it yet.

Now it happened that some years ago The Parish changed its priest.
A fella came from Wexford to the heathens in the East
And his first religious exercise (before he knelt to pray)
Was to visit his parishioners and have a cup o' tay!

He visited big houses and he visited the small
And some he didn't fancy so he didn't call at all
But the house of Sean and Bernie was the last one on his list
So he marched up to the front door an' battered wi' his fist.

When Sean appeared he shouted (for this priest was quite a rogue)
'My name is Father Murphy – but I'm not from Boolavogue!' –
Sean put his fingers to his lips and looked about to cry.
'For God's sake, father, houl yer whisht! It's the 12th day of July!'

The priest looked round in some surprise as Sean led him down the
    hall
For pictures of King Billy decorated every wall
In living room and kitchen there were several more 'King Billys'
And a bowl upon the table top was full of orange lilies.

There were Union Jacks and Ulster flags and orange sashes too
The bunting strung across the room was all red, white and blue
Red, white and blue were everywhere (with never a touch of green)
And smilin' from the mantelpiece was a photo of the Queen!

Sean grinned and said, 'Now, father, I can see your consternation!
Here, have a drop of Bushmills and you'll hear the explanation
I don't know what you'll think of it or how you will receive it
And I really couldn't blame you if you say you don't believe it!

We bought this house ten years ago and the night that we moved in
We were hangin' holy pictures when we heard an awful din!
From the wall around us came the music of 'The Sash'
And the pictures all fell off the walls and landed with a crash!

I was hanging up His Holiness at the head of Jimmy's bed
When the hammer turned itself around and hit me on the head
I found myself being strangled with a yard of picture wire
And the Holy Water flew across and put out the kitchen fire!

Well, we didn't stop to argue – we were out the door like hell
And we spent that night and several more in the nearest cheap hotel
We had a ghost or poltergeist – there was no two ways about it
But on one thing we both agreed – we'd rather be without it!

Well, we thought we'd get a medium in and see what that would do
'Jobs wanted' in the 'Tele Ads' – we scanned them through and
     through.
At last I shouted 'Bernie! I've found just what we need!'
It says 'Medium – Madame Jacqueline, satisfaction guaranteed!'

Well, Madame Jacqueline arrived – on a bike from Cullybacky
Saying 'I am Madame Jacqueline – but me Mammy calls me Jackie!
Now take me to this ghost of yours – be it orange, white or green
I'll teach the same boy not to mess wi' Madame Jacqueline!'

We sat her down inside the house and she went into a trance
(After several double vodkas which she ordered in advance)
I whispered, 'Bernie! This is mad! The whole thing's a disaster!'
Says Bernie, 'Whist, she's in a trance!'
Says I, 'The woman's plastered!'

Well, after half an hour she woke up and looked around.
She says 'Now listen here to me and I'll tell you what I've found!
The ghostie's name is Willie John and this is what he said,
"You don't stop bein' an Orangeman
Just because you're dead!"

Well, it seems he lived here years ago and it gets under his skin
To think that 'Prods' is movin' out, 'left footers' movin' in,
But still in spite of bein' wrong, he thinks you're not too bad
So he's come up with a compromise although it makes him sad.

The agreement is that every '12th' before yes bite or sup
The holy pictures all come down and the 'King Billys' all come up
The bunting of red, white and blue is strung across the hall
And the picture of his Holiness is turned to face the wall.

As well (on the eleventh night) as part of his yearly 'bash'
He'll be allowed to play the flute, and he'll only play 'The Sash'
If you agree to all these things you've nothing left to fear,
You'll be left in peace to lead your lives, except for once a year.'

'Well that's the story father, believe it if you please.
We keep to the agreement and we live here at our ease,
And listening to his oul' orange flute's a thing we quite enjoy,
And last year he gave up 'The Sash' and played 'The Minstrel Boy!'
And here's your hat now, father, for I see you're movin' on
But if we had to have a ghost, there's worse nor Willie John!'

Crawford Howard